The Blood of Jesus

Blood
Power

DAG HEWARD-MILLS

Parchment House

Unless otherwise stated, all Scripture quotations are taken from the King James Version of the Bible.

BLOOD POWER

Copyright © 2014 Dag Heward-Mills

First published 2014 by Parchment House
20th Printing 2019

[77]Find out more about Dag Heward Mills at:

Healing Jesus Campaign
Email: evangelist@daghewardmills.org
Website: www.daghewardmills.org
Facebook: Dag Heward-Mills
Twitter: @EvangelistDag

ISBN : 978-1-61395-482-9

Contents

CHAPTER 1

The Words and
the Blood of Jesus Christ

There are many things to learn from Jesus Christ. There are many things we can study about Jesus Christ! We could study His life, His family, His achievements, His ministry, His travels, His goals and His leadership style. But the two most important things about Jesus Christ are His words and His blood.

Precious Words

The words of Jesus are important because they teach us the truths and the wisdom of God.

It is enough to place the words of Jesus above all human words. Today, the words of Jesus are separated from the rest of scripture by red ink.

Formerly, the beautiful words of Christ were indiscriminately mingled with the rest of Scripture. Modern Bibles assign the deserved honour to the words of Jesus. In red-letter bibles, the words of Jesus are placed in a class of their own; a class without equal.

At the Reformation stage of the church, men focused on the work of Christ on Calvary. Earlier, the person of Christ was the focus of attention. In later years, the details of *His earthly life* from the manger to the cross became the focus of intense study. Today, we must also emphasize the blood of Jesus Christ.

Fortunately, the unique value of the blood of Jesus is being recognized today. The blood of Jesus is being assigned the distinction it deserves.

Precious Blood

Our sins cannot be washed away by the words of Jesus. We need the blood of Jesus to wash us from our wretchedness and sinful state so that our names can be written in the Book of Life. No matter how much Jesus spoke, preached and taught, He still needed to rescue us by the power of His blood. Without the shedding of blood there is no remission of sins! There needed to be shedding of blood so that our sins could be covered.

Who Would Pay for Our Sins?

It is true that the preaching and wisdom of God is found in the teachings of Jesus Christ. But who would pay for our sins? Who would pay the price for us to escape from hell? We are redeemed (bought back) by the blood of Jesus Christ. We were redeemed not by the words of Jesus but by His blood. We were redeemed not by the blood of bulls and goats but by the blood of Jesus.

Stop Preaching and Let the Blood Flow

Why did Jesus Christ stop preaching at the age of thirty-three and head for the cross? Why did He not continue His mission of preaching and teaching the word of God in other countries? Could He not have gone to Syria, Lebanon, England, Germany, Iraq, Persia, India and Africa? Certainly He could have! He was only thirty-three years old when he gave his life on the cross. If he had lived another forty years, of perhaps to the age of eighty, He would have been able to travel throughout the whole world.

When I visited Chennai in India, I found a church that was built in memory of St Thomas, the doubter. Thomas was one of the twelve apostles of Jesus Christ. Apparently, Thomas the apostle had travelled to India and ministered there. He was martyred there and the church was built there in his honour. If Thomas, who lived and walked with Jesus was able to travel to India then Jesus Himself would have been able to travel to India as well. It was well within the capacity of Jesus Christ to travel all around the world and preach the gospel of the kingdom.

Jesus Christ stopped preaching suddenly and made His way to Jerusalem where He knew He would be captured, tortured and murdered. Jesus said, 'No one takes my life from me. I lay it down of my own accord.' Why did Jesus do that? Was He thinking correctly?

Why the Cross?

Why did Jesus willingly and consciously go to the place of His crucifixion where evil men would put Him to death? This was the way Jesus allowed His blood to be shed for the sins of mankind. If Jesus had not shed His blood for us, His ministry would have lasted until His message would have faded away. Today, the power of the shed blood of Jesus is still at work. It reaches to the highest mountain and to the lowest valley of our world. God's power of salvation is released even two thousand years after the death of Jesus Christ because of the blood of Jesus. This is why the blood of Jesus is important.

The Words of Jesus

We would not know that Jesus is the way, the truth and the life if He had not spoken these famous words. Salvation would not have come to us if Jesus had not told us that God so loved the world, that He gave His only begotten Son, that whoever believes in Him shall not perish, but have eternal life.

And that God did not send the Son into the world to judge the world, but that the world might be saved through Him.

3

Even though we are washed by the blood of Jesus, our knowledge of God and our knowledge of the way of salvation come through the famous words of Jesus. It is Jesus who said, the thief comes only to steal and kill and destroy; I came that they may have life, and have it abundantly. We would not have known where to go and what to do if Jesus had not said, Come to Me, all who are weary and heavy-laden, and I will give you rest. Take My yoke upon you and learn from Me, for I am gentle and humble in heart, and you will find rest for your souls. It is through the comprehensive package of the blood of Jesus and the words of Jesus that salvation has come to men.

The words of Jesus are important because they make us understand salvation and make us wise. But His blood is even more important because we are not saved when we are wise! But we are not saved when we understand things and we understand the wisdom of God. We are saved when our sins are washed away by the blood of Jesus.

CHAPTER 2

Why the Blood of Jesus
is Precious Blood

Forasmuch as ye know that ye were not redeemed with
CORRUPTIBLE THINGS, AS SILVER AND GOLD,
from your vain conversation received by tradition
from your fathers; But with THE PRECIOUS
BLOOD OF CHRIST, as of a lamb without blemish
and without spot:

1 Peter 1:18-19

But Christ being come an high priest of good things to
come, by a greater and more perfect tabernacle, not
made with hands, that is to say, not of this building;
nither by the blood of goats and calves, but by his
own blood he entered in once into the holy place,
having obtained eternal redemption for us. For if
the BLOOD OF BULLS AND OF GOATS, and the
ashes of an heifer sprinkling the unclean, sanctifieth
to the purifying of the flesh: How much more shall
THE BLOOD OF CHRIST, who through the eternal
Spirit offered himself without spot to God, purge your
conscience from dead works to serve the living God?

Hebrews 9:11-14

Theblood of Jesus is precious, because it is superior to
all other kinds of blood. There are many other kinds of
blood the bible speaks of. But none of these has any
power to save, heal or deliver anyone. Have you ever heard of
anyone's blood being able to wash sins away? Never! Nothing
can wash away our sins except the blood of Jesus Christ. Notice
several different kinds of blood that the bible speaks about. None
of these can compare with the blood of Jesus Christ, the Lamb of
God which taketh away the sins of the whole world.

Other people's blood may have a message and may have some
power. The blood of Abel, for instance, spoke of murder and
cried for revenge. And to Jesus the mediator of the new covenant,
and to the blood of sprinkling, that speaketh better things than
that of Abel" (Hebrews 12:24). But the blood of Jesus Christ
spoke about better things and had a far greater power.

The blood of saints and prophets calls out for punishment to
be meted out to those who do not fear God (Revelation 16:6).
The blood of bulls and goats is blood that is powerless to bring
forgiveness (Hebrews 10:4).

Shedding the blood of the children of Israel would probably
result in some kind of punishment from God. Shedding the blood
of martyrs, saints and prophets would also come with its own
specific judgment. The blood of saints, prophets and martyrs
does have some significance. But only the blood of Jesus can
save you from your sins. That is why this book is all about the
blood of Jesus Christ and not the blood of anyone else.

Other Types of Blood That Cannot Save Anyone

1. The blood of Abel

That upon you may come all the righteous blood shed
upon the earth, from the BLOOD OF righteous ABEL ...
whom ye slew between the temple and the altar.

Matthew 23:35

2. The blood of saints and prophets

For they have shed the BLOOD OF SAINTS AND PROPHETS, and thou hast given them blood to drink; for they are worthy.

Revelation 16:6

3. The blood of bulls and goats

For it is not possible that the BLOOD OF BULLS AND OF GOATS should take away sins.

Hebrews 10:4

4. The blood of martyrs

And I saw the woman drunken with the blood of the saints, and with the BLOOD OF THE MARTYRS of Jesus: and when I saw her, I wondered with great admiration.

Revelation 17:6

5. The blood of servants

Rejoice, O ye nations, with his people: for he will avenge the BLOOD OF HIS SERVANTS, and will render vengeance to his adversaries, and will be merciful unto his land, and to his people.

Deuteronomy 32:43

6. The blood of princes

Ye shall eat the flesh of the mighty, and drink the BLOOD OF THE PRINCES of the earth, of rams, of lambs, and of goats, of bullocks, all of them fatlings of Bashan.

Ezekiel 39:18

7. The blood of the children of Israel

Because thou hast had a perpetual hatred, and hast shed the BLOOD OF THE CHILDREN OF ISRAEL by the force of the sword in the time of their calamity, in the time that their iniquity had an end:

Ezekiel 35:5

8. The blood of Zacharias

That upon you may come all the righteous blood shed upon the earth, from the blood of righteous Abel unto the BLOOD OF ZACHARIAS son of Barachias, whom ye slew between the temple and the altar.

Matthew 23:35

9. The blood of innocents

Because they have forsaken me, and have estranged this place, and have burned incense in it unto other gods, whom neither they nor their fathers have known, nor the kings of Judah, and have filled this place with the BLOOD OF INNOCENTS;

Jeremiah 19:4

10. The blood of the just

For the sins of her prophets, and the iniquities of her priests, that have shed THE BLOOD OF THE JUST in the midst of her

Lamentations 4:13

11. The blood of the wicked

The righteous shall rejoice when he seeth the vengeance: he shall wash his feet in the BLOOD OF THE WICKED.

Psalms 58:10

12. The blood of war

Moreover thou knowest also what Joab the son of Zeruiah did to me, and what he did to the two captains of the hosts of Israel, unto Abner the son of Ner, and unto Amasa the son of Jether, whom he slew, and shed the blood of war in peace, and put THE BLOOD OF WAR upon his girdle that was about his loins, and in his shoes that were on his feet.

1 Kings 2:5

13. The blood of Naboth

And thou shalt speak unto him, saying, Thus saith the LORD, Hast thou killed, and also taken possession? And thou shalt speak unto him, saying, Thus saith the LORD, In the place where dogs licked the BLOOD OF NABOTH shall dogs lick thy blood, even thine.

1 Kings 21:19

Surely I have seen yesterday the BLOOD OF NABOTH, and the blood of his sons, saith the LORD; and I will requite thee in this plat, saith the LORD. Now therefore take and cast him into the plat of ground, according to the word of the LORD.

2 Kings 9:26

14. The blood of the scapegoat

And he shall go out unto the altar that is before the LORD, and make an atonement for it; and shall take of the blood of the bullock, and of the BLOOD OF THE GOAT, and put it upon the horns of the altar round about. And he shall sprinkle of the blood upon it with his finger seven times, and cleanse it, and hallow it from the uncleanness of the children of Israel. And when he hath made an end of reconciling the holy place, and the tabernacle of the congregation, and the altar, he shall bring the live goat: And Aaron shall lay both his hands upon the head of the live goat, and confess over him all the iniquities of the children of Israel, and all their transgressions in all their sins, putting them upon the head of the goat, and shall send him away by the hand of a fit man into the wilderness: And the goat shall bear upon him all their iniquities unto a land not inhabited: and he shall let go the goat in the wilderness.

Leviticus 16:18-22

15. The blood of Abner – the price for David's throne.

And afterward when David heard it, he said, I and my kingdom are guiltless before the LORD for ever from THE BLOOD OF ABNER the son of Ner:

2 Samuel 3:28

CHAPTER 3

How the Blood of Jesus Acquired its Importance

1. **God revealed the importance of blood through the prophet Moses and therefore commanded that blood should not be eaten.**

   For the life of the flesh is in the blood: and I have given it to you upon the altar to make an atonement for your souls: for it is the blood that maketh an atonement for the soul. therefore I said unto the children of Israel, NO SOUL OF YOU SHALL EAT BLOOD,

   Leviticus 17:11-12

The generation that lived in the time of Moses would not have known about the importance of blood. Perhaps they would have thought that it was the heart, the brain or the kidneys that were important. But through the teaching of Moses, they learnt that the life of a person is in his blood. All the other parts of the body could be eaten but the blood was not supposed to be eaten because it represented a life.

2. **Long before medical science discovered it, Moses taught us that the blood of a person contained his life.**

   For the life of the flesh is in the blood: ...

   Leviticus 17:11

   Today, we know that the blood carries life to all parts of the body. Moses could not have known that by medical science. He knew this because God revealed it to him. Life is in the blood!

The Race for Blood

One night, I was on duty at the emergency ward when a young man was brought to the hospital. This gentleman had an unusual problem in which he was vomiting blood uncontrollably. He retched and vomited all night long. Each time he vomited, He brought out bright red blood. He did not vomit any food. His stomach was empty and he was bringing out pure blood. By 2.00am his condition began to deteriorate because he had lost so much blood.

I walked to and fro from the blood bank that night, fetching blood for this man. I was trying to bring him back from the dead. It was a race for life. By the morning the space around his bed was covered with bright red blood because he had vomited all around him all night long. Sad to say, in the end we were unable to prevent him from going to the grave because he had brought out more blood than we were able to replace.

The race that night was a race to get as much blood to the man quickly enough. Only the blood could prevent the man from dying and going to the grave.

Indeed, the race today is the race to get the blood of Jesus to as many places as possible quickly enough.

3. **Because the blood *contains* the life of a person, it represents his life.**

   For it is the life of all flesh; the blood of it is for the life thereof: ...

   Leviticus 17:14

If all your blood were to drain out, you would probably have a bowl of blood. A bowl of human blood therefore represents a human life. A bowl of goat blood represents the goat's life. A bowl of elephants blood represents the elephant's life. The bowlful of the blood of the Jesus that flowed down on the cross therefore represented the life of the Son of God. He gave His life and we saw it when His blood flowed out. This is what we mean when we say that Jesus Christ gave His life for us. It meant that He gave His blood! To give your life is to give your blood! To give your blood is to give your life!

4. **The blood has been chosen by God as the only thing that can be offered to appease Him and to atone for sin.**

   For the life of the flesh is in the blood: and I HAVE GIVEN IT TO YOU UPON THE ALTAR TO MAKE AN ATONEMENT FOR YOUR SOULS: ...

Leviticus 17:11

5. **The New Testament confirms that only 'blood' can save you.**

   And almost all things are by the law purged with blood; and without shedding of blood is no remission.

Hebrews 9:22

Thus, this great truth about life in the blood revealed to Moses has passed on to Paul and the New Testament church. The apostle Paul makes it abundantly clear that without the shedding of blood (without the giving of a life) no one can be saved. You have to give a life to get a life. You have to shed the blood to save and redeem lives.

What Can Wash Away the Stains?

Many years ago, my mother showed me something that I never forgot. She picked out one of my father's shirts and pointed to a stain in it.

"Do you know what these stains are? These are stains from coconut water. Your father likes coconuts so much and he is always drinking coconut water."

She said, "So many of his shirts are stained with this coconut water and I cannot get rid of them."

She explained, "I can wash away everything with soap. I can wash out palm oil, dirt, chocolate, tea, coffee, stew, soup, toothpaste but I cannot wash out coconut stain."

"Wow,' I said, "I never knew that coconut stains were so difficult to get rid of."

Indeed, key soap, blue Omo, Ariel, Duck soap, Sunlight soap, Rexona, Lux, Imperial Leather were not able to wash away those coconut stains.

"So what can wash away the coconut stain?"

"Nothing," she said.

Every time I think of the coconut stain I think of the stain of sin.

I ask myself, "What can wash away our sins? What can wash away our lies, our stealing, our fornication and our murders?" Nothing really can wipe away what we have done in the past.

Only the blood of Jesus. God's word teaches us that the blood of Jesus does have power to wipe away the stain of our past sins.

Nothing but the blood of Jesus can wash away our sins. Nothing but the blood of Jesus!!

Only the blood of Jesus has the power to wash away these terrible stains.

CHAPTER 4

How the Blood of Jesus Has Performed the Greatest Miracle

The greatest miracle is the miracle of salvation.

HOW SHALL WE ESCAPE, IF WE NEGLECT SO GREAT SALVATION; which at the first began to be spoken by the Lord, and was confirmed unto us by them that heard him;

Hebrews 2:3

S alvation is the greatest miracle because it is a combination of seven fantastic experiences. Each of these experiences is an amazing and incredible event. The seven experiences of salvation are clear. These are all fantastic miracles that would not happen naturally.

Seven Experiences of Salvation

a. Salvation involves you being forgiven.

b. Salvation involves the record of your sins being wiped away

c. Salvation involves being loved as you are.

d. Salvation involves your release from prison and captivity.

e. Salvation involves a light shining in your darkness.

f. Salvation involves your going to heaven.

g. Salvation involves you getting to know Jesus Christ.

1. Salvation is the greatest miracle because it is a miracle for anyone to be forgiven.

Come now, and let us reason together, saith the Lord: though your sins be as scarlet, they shall be as white as snow; though they be red like crimson, they shall be as wool.

Isaiah 1:18

There was a man who came home and found his wife in bed with another man. He was very angry with his wife. When he reported this to the pastors they all expected that he would divorce his wife. To everyone's amazement, he did not divorce his wife but rather forgave her and warned her not do that again. This was a big surprise to the entire church family. It was indeed a great miracle for the husband to forgive his wife, even after catching her in the very act.

This lady experienced the miracle of forgiveness from her husband. This is the miracle that converts something that is red as scarlet to become as white as snow.

2. **Salvation is the greatest miracle because it is always a miracle for your sins to be wiped away.**

Come now, and let us reason together, saith the Lord: though your sins be as scarlet, they shall be as white as snow; though they be red like crimson, they shall be as wool.

Isaiah 1:18

Heaven is a place where there are no more records of your failures and mistakes. When you are forgiven and the record of your sins is wiped away, it is as if you never sinned. In our world today, the records of any past criminal activity is never wiped away. If you commit any sin it remains recorded on the internet forever. Human beings decide never to forget what you have done. Today, there is a movement which is fighting for the right to be forgotten. Through the right to be forgotten, they are asking that records of certain things should be removed from the internet. *WE* are not fighting for the right to be forgotten through the blood of Jesus! We are receiving pardon and the records are being washed away mercifully.

When you have been a criminal, there are always forms to fill which call up your past sins and mistakes. It is indeed a great blessing to have your sins washed away and the records changed forever. Through the blood of Jesus, your sins will be washed away and though they were red like crimson they become white as wool. There is no more record.

3. **Salvation is the greatest miracle because it is always a miracle for someone to love a person who has many problems.**

But God commendeth his love toward us, in that, while we were yet sinners, Christ died for us.

Romans 5:8

In our world today, it is a miracle for someone with serious deformities to find a spouse. I once saw a man who had fallen in love with a crippled lady. It was a miracle because she could not do anything to help herself. Why would someone marry a person with such deformities and obvious handicaps? This is the question you must ask Jesus Christ. Why?

Why would He come towards us and even desire to be close to people with such complex failings? But God has demonstrated His love towards us by doing the greatest miracle ever: salvation! While we are yet sinners, full of evil, full of wickedness and full of defects, He loves us. This is the greatest miracle! The salvation of wicked sinners!

4. **Salvation is the greatest miracle because it is always a miracle for someone to be released from prison.**

The Spirit of the Lord is upon me, because he hath anointed me to preach the gospel to the poor; he hath sent me to heal the brokenhearted, TO PREACH DELIVERANCE TO THE CAPTIVES, and recovering of sight to the blind, to set at liberty them that are bruised.

Luke 4:18

I once met a prisoner who touched my heart. This man was a convicted murderer. He was in prison for life because he had murdered his own son. His fervency, zeal and prayer life touched me so much that I wanted him to be released from prison. Try as I did, I could not think of any way to get him out of the prison. The prison gates were heavily guarded and there were armed solders everywhere, so I quickly discarded the idea of helping him escape.

I thought about getting a presidential pardon for this man. But I did not know the president, nor did I know anyone who knew the president. As I left the prison that day, I looked at this prayerful prisoner and thought to myself, "it is going to take a miracle to get you out of here."

Indeed, it will take a miracle to get the souls of this world out of the prison. To be saved is to be set free from captivity. Today, if salvation has come to you, the great miracle of being set free from prison has happened to you. Salvation is the greatest miracle.

5. **Salvation is the greatest miracle because it is always a great miracle for light to shine into the darkness.**

THE PEOPLE THAT WALKED IN DARKNESS HAVE SEEN A GREAT LIGHT: they that dwell in the land of the shadow of death, upon them hath the light shined.

Isaiah 9:2

It is a great miracle for light to come into a person's life. Light is a miracle. When the light shines into the darkness, a great miracle has taken place. For lights to come on in a country there must be a dam or a massive power plant.

Great technology, scientific discoveries and lots of money must be deployed to turn the lights on in a dark country. That is why there are still many countries that do not have electricity today. It takes a miracle for the lights to come on. If salvation has appeared to you, a light has shone in the darkness of your soul. Believe me, God has shown mercy to you and done a great miracle in your life! Surely, salvation must be the greatest miracle.

6. **Salvation is the greatest miracle because it is a great miracle for you to go to heaven.**

And one of the elders answered, saying unto me, what are these which are arrayed in white robes? And WHENCE CAME THEY?

And I said unto him, Sir, thou knowest. And he said to me, these are they which came out of great tribulation, and have washed their robes, and made them white in the blood of the Lamb.

Revelation 7:13-14

Even in this world there are places that you will never go to. Will you ever walk in the Kremlin, in the White House or in the Head of State's bedroom? Not likely! If you were ever to walk in the Oval Office of the White House, it would be a miracle. But heaven is even greater than the Oval Office of the White House. It would be a great miracle for you to ever walk on those streets of gold.

If you ever have the chance to walk on the streets of gold, you would have experienced a great miracle. Today, if God is giving you an entrance to heaven, a great miracle has taken place. Think about how bad you are, how full of sin and how full of evil you are. How could somebody as lowly as I ever find his way into a place like heaven? That must be a miracle! For somebody like you to be welcomed into heaven is a great miracle indeed! This is why your salvation is the greatest miracle on earth.

7. Salvation is the greatest miracle because it is a great miracle for you to know Jesus.

Wherefore, my brethren, ye also are become dead to the law by the body of Christ; THAT YE SHOULD BE MARRIED TO ANOTHER, *EVEN* TO HIM who is raised from the dead, that we should bring forth fruit unto God.

Romans 7:4

Today, God is giving you the great privilege of coming close to the Prince of Peace and the Lord of Lords.

Finding salvation is finding Jesus Christ. There are certain people you will never meet in your life.

It is not likely that you will ever meet the president of China or the Prime Minister of England. To meet any of these people would be a great miracle indeed. The other day, I spoke to the president of a certain country. That was a great miracle because there was no way that this president would ever have had a phone conversation with me.

Even on earth, you never thought you would marry the prince. It would be such a miracle to be married to the prince, to live with him, to stay with him, to bath with him and to eat with him. What an amazing privilege it would be to even meet the prince!

To meet Jesus Christ is an even greater miracle. To be married to Christ is unthinkable. You never thought you would be married to Christ. Isn't it? But the bible teaches us that when we are saved we are married to Christ.

CHAPTER 5

How the Blood of Jesus Gives Life

For the life of the flesh is in the blood….

Leviticus 17:11

1. Blood was created to carry life.

Then Jesus said unto them, Verily, verily, I say unto you, Except ye eat the flesh of the Son of man, and DRINK HIS BLOOD, YE HAVE NO LIFE IN YOU"

John 6:53

Blood is a red, oxygen-containing liquid that gives life to everything it comes in contact with. Just as human blood carries life to every part of the body, the blood of Jesus carries eternal life everywhere it goes. Blood carries life by carrying life-giving oxygen everywhere and taking away poisonous carbon dioxide.

The Life is in the Blood

One day I watched a man's leg being amputated in the theatre. Never had I felt such depression as I watched the operation unfold. I felt very sorry for the man as I watched his leg being carried away by hospital attendants. But a week later, I found this man whose leg was amputated sitting up in his bed, smiling and laughing with visitors. A few days later, I saw him going home happily. He still had life in him because he still had blood in him.

He still had life in him and was going home to continue living happily ever after with his family. You see, the life is in the blood! The life is not in the legs or the arms! If the life was in his legs, he would have died when they cut it off. Actually, the life is in the blood! When a person's blood drains out of him, he dies because his life has drained out of him.

2. The Blood gives life because it can reach every part of the body.

After this I beheld, and, lo, a great multitude, which no man could number, of ALL NATIONS, AND KINDREDS, AND PEOPLE, and tongues, stood before the throne, and before the Lamb, clothed with white robes, and palms in their hands; ...And one of the elders answered, saying unto me, What are these

which are arrayed in white robes? And whence came they? And I said unto him, Sir, thou knowest. And he said to me, these are they which came out of great tribulation, and have washed their robes, and MADE THEM WHITE IN THE BLOOD OF THE LAMB

Revelation 7:9, 13-14

Just as our human blood by its fluid nature reaches every part of the body, the blood of Jesus Christ can reach every single member of the body of Christ.

The blood gives life because it unites the whole body. It unites the rest of the body with vital organs like the heart and the lungs. Just as our human blood unites the entire body, all members of the body are related to one another and to the head by the blood that flows everywhere. Through the blood of Jesus, everyone can be connected to the head, that is God.

Just as the blood reaches every part of the body, the blood of Jesus is able to reach every part of the world. The blood of Jesus is effective universally. Every tribe and every nation of the world can been reached by this blood. The blood of Jesus will connect the remotest village in the world to the throne of God. The lamb of God that takes away the sins of the world no matter which part of the world.

The blood of Jesus is therefore the basis for strong relations and bonds that develop in the body of Christ between apparently unrelated people of varied backgrounds.

3. **The blood carries life because it has the ability to carry nourishment.**

   Whoso eateth my flesh, and DRINKETH MY BLOOD, HATH ETERNAL LIFE; and I will raise him up at the last day. For my flesh is meat indeed, and my blood is drink indeed.

John 6:54-55

Blood is a red liquid, containing dissolved food that gives life to everything it comes in contact with. Just as human blood brings food to every part of the body, the blood of Jesus Christ brings life and well-being to everyone it comes in contact with. Within the blood are molecules of life-giving protein, carbohydrates, fats, vitamins and minerals. No wonder there is life in the blood!

Anyone who eats and drinks the blood of Jesus is going to enjoy eternal life!

4. **The blood gives life because it has the ability to cleanse you regularly.**

   But if we walk in the light, as he is in the light, we have fellowship one with another, and the BLOOD of Jesus Christ his Son CLEANSETH us from all sin. If we confess our sins, he is faithful and just to forgive us our sins, and to cleanse us from all unrighteousness

   1 John 1:7,9

   Blood is a red, carbon dioxide removing liquid that gives life to everything it comes in contact with. Just as human blood carries away unwanted carbon dioxide, and disposes of it in the lungs, the blood of Jesus carries away our sin and filthiness. The blood of Jesus is a sin-removing liquid that is flowing from Calvary's cross to the whole world.

5. **The blood gives life because it has the ability to purge and to sanctify.**

   WHEREFORE JESUS ALSO, THAT HE MIGHT SANCTIFY THE PEOPLE WITH HIS OWN BLOOD, suffered without the gate. Let us go forth therefore unto him without the camp, bearing his reproach

   Hebrews 13:12-13

   Blood is a red liquid that removes deadly poisons from the body. Human blood also carries away unwanted poisonous chemicals like urea and disposes of them through the kidney.

These deadly poisons are removed by the blood and dumped in the kidney so that they come out in your urine.

Everything that comes out of your urine was once in your blood. All your urine was once a part of your blood. Imagine how bad-smelling your blood and body would be if it did not come out of you.

Blood therefore gives life to everything it comes in contact with by removing deadly poisons. Indeed, the blood of Jesus removes the deadly and poisonous sins from our lives.

The blood of Jesus washes away poisonous and dangerous sins, attitudes and stains from our lives. The blood of Jesus keeps you away from death by removing poisons from your life. The blood of Jesus is what keeps you from eternal death and hell.

6. The blood gives life because it destroys diseases.

And I heard a loud voice saying in heaven, Now is come salvation, and strength, and the kingdom of our God, and the power of his Christ: for the accuser of our brethren is cast down, which accused them before our God day and night. AND THEY OVERCAME HIM BY THE BLOOD OF THE LAMB, and by the word of their testimony; and they loved not their lives unto the death.

Revelation 12:10-11

Blood is a red, liquid containing cells that fight diseases, infections and other evils that can kill the body. This is why blood gives life to everything it comes in contact with. We overcome infection through the white blood cells in blood. Through blood, we fight battles against germs and other invaders. Through the blood of Jesus we overcome the devil and other invading evil spirits.

Blood is a red, liquid containing special cells called platelets that bring healing to injured parts of the body. Blood heals. Just as the platelets and other clotting factors within the blood help to form clots and plugs in wounds, the blood of Jesus helps our wounds to heal.

Through the blood of Jesus we are forgiven from our terrible sins and receive the inspiration to forgive others and overcome bitterness.

You can overcome physical diseases and spiritual diseases through the blood of Jesus. Spiritual diseases like bitterness, jealousy, hatred and insecurity can be overcome through the blood of Jesus.

CHAPTER 6

Salvation through the Blood

Through the blood of Jesus salvation has come to the world. The scripture reveals five different steps that are taken on the road to salvation through the blood of Jesus.

1. The first step to salvation is FORGIVENESS THROUGH THE BLOOD.

In whom we have redemption THROUGH HIS BLOOD, THE FORGIVENESS OF SINS, according to the riches of his grace; wherein he hath abounded toward us in all wisdom and prudence.

Ephesians 1:7-8

Through the blood of Jesus you receive the first step towards your salvation – forgiveness. Forgiveness means that God has stopped feeling angry about you. He has pardoned you and written off your debts. You are discharged from your obligation and God is no more resentful towards you.

The Blood versus The Orange Juice

I once worked with someone on an important project. He was a great assistant and worked very hard. One day, our church was preparing for its grand dedication. This gentleman was in charge of the preparation. It was a crucial and very significant moment in my ministry. Everything hinged on him doing his work.

One day, I came to the church building site and found that this gentleman was not around. I asked where he was, because I had repeatedly emphasized to him that he needed to finish the work in time for the programme. To my shock this gentleman had left the country and abandoned me in mid-air. I was launched into a terrible crisis and had to organise several alternative emergency measures to save myself from a terrible disgrace and embarrassment. I was very upset with the gentleman because I had given myself to work with him and had trusted him greatly. After the programme I decided not to work with him any more.

One day, I was at home when a delegation arrived in my house. This was a delegation that had come on the behalf of this gentleman to plead for me to forgive him and accept him to continue working for me. I listened to all that they had to say. At the end of their speech they presented me with a basket that contained some orange juice and apple juice.

As I looked at the basket I smiled to myself because I remembered the blood of Jesus. These people were trying to wipe out the sins of this man with the orange juice and apple juice. But orange juice cannot wash away sins. Only the blood of Jesus can wash away sins. I forgave him, and accepted him back smiling to myself every time I drank some of their orange juice. Perhaps that is how God feels when He sees the blood of Jesus and has to forgive and pardon our sins. There is forgiveness in the blood.

2. The second step to salvation is CLEANSING THROUGH THE BLOOD.

But if we walk in the light, as he is in the light, we have fellowship one with another, and the BLOOD OF JESUS CHRIST HIS SON CLEANSETH us from all sin….

1 John 1:7

After being forgiven you need cleansing. This process takes you one-step further than forgiveness did. You may be forgiven but there is often a scent of the past evils that we were involved with.

The Armed Robber Who Needed Cleansing

One day, a young man was being chased by a crowd who suspected that he was an armed robber. Unfortunately, he fell into a huge watery septic tank. This young man could not swim in the swirling stew of faeces. He screamed for help and someone stretched a rod out to him. He was pulled out and saved from an ignominious death. He stood by the pool, thankful just to be alive. After a while, someone said to him, "You better go and have a bath. Your life has been saved but you are still smelling!" And with that the young man was ushered away for a thorough disinfecting bath. Although he was saved from death he needed a serious clean-up.

That is how salvation is. Though you are forgiven for your sins there is a need for you to be cleansed.

3. The third step to salvation is SANCTIFICATION THROUGH THE BLOOD.

For the bodies of those beasts, whose blood is brought into the sanctuary by the high priest for sin, are burned without the camp. Wherefore Jesus also, that he might SANCTIFY THE PEOPLE WITH HIS OWN BLOOD, suffered without the gate. Let us go forth therefore unto him without the camp, bearing his reproach

Hebrews 13:11-13

Sanctification takes you even further than forgiveness and cleansing do. It means you have been set apart for a sacred religious purpose. It is only the sanctifying power of the blood of Jesus that can move you so far from your past evil state. This is the power that can utterly transform a criminal into a priest of God! This power is the sanctifying power of the blood of Jesus.

Peter called himself "elect" according to the sanctification of the spirit and sprinkling of the blood. "Elect according to the foreknowledge of God the father, through sanctification of the spirit, unto obedience and sprinkling of the blood of Jesus Christ: grace unto you, and peace, be multiplied" (1 Peter 1:2). He had been elevated from being a fisherman to becoming the head of the worldwide church. How did that happen? It happened through the sanctifying power of the blood of Jesus.

4. The fourth step to salvation is REDEMPTION THROUGH THE BLOOD.

And they sung a new song, saying, Thou art worthy to take the book, and to open the seals thereof: for thou wast slain, and HAST REDEEMED US TO GOD BY THY BLOOD out of every kindred, and tongue, and people, and nation; And hast made us unto our God kings and priests: and we shall reign on the earth.

Revelation 5:9-10

In whom we have REDEMPTION THROUGH HIS BLOOD, the forgiveness of sins, according to the riches of his grace.

Ephesians 1:7

The next step in the process of salvation is to be redeemed. To redeem is to get, to win, or to buy someone or something back. To redeem means to buy back a slave. Christ has legally bought us back from the devil's slave camp. He paid for us with His blood. *When God went shopping, He decided to buy you back to Him and He paid the bill with His blood.*

We all use things that we have not bought. You may hire a car instead of buying it. You may hire a dress without buying it. You may live in a house without buying it. God could have related with us without buying us back to Him. God has, however, decided to forgive us and to buy us back from the devil! He wants to have a permanent relationship with us.

When God buys you from the devil's slave camp, you belong to him permanently. Your forgiveness, your cleansing and your sanctification are permanent. You belong to God. The devil cannot make any more claims to your life. Your life has been paid for with the blood.

5. The fifth step to salvation is RECONCILIATION THROUGH THE BLOOD.

For all have sinned, and come short of the glory of God; Being justified freely by his grace through the redemption that is in Christ Jesus: Whom God hath set forth to be A PROPITIATION THROUGH FAITH IN HIS BLOOD, to declare his righteousness for the remission of sins that are past, through the forbearance of God; To declare, I say, at this time his righteousness: that he might be just, and the justifier of him which believeth in Jesus.

Romans 3:23-26

Another great blessing that come to us through the blood of Jesus is reconciliation. Final reconciliation with God comes because you are forgiven, cleansed, sanctified and redeemed. You can now enjoy a reconciled relationship with God. This is what propitiation is all about.

Propitiation involves a regaining of the favour and the goodwill that you lost with God. Through the blood of Jesus you will appease the heavenly Father and restore your relationship with Him.

CHAPTER 7

The Supernatural Abilities of the Blood

The blood of Jesus Christ has supernatural power. Through the blood of Jesus, major spiritual changes take place in your life. None of these changes are natural. Every change that comes about in your life through the blood of Jesus is supernatural. Most people are aware of the supernatural power of the Holy Spirit. Many people speak of the supernatural power of angels. Some people know about the supernatural power of Jehovah. But few people know about the supernatural power of the blood of Jesus. Indeed, there is great supernatural power in the blood of our Saviour.

1. **The blood of Jesus has supernatural power that never expires.**

    Forasmuch as ye know that ye were not REDEEMED with corruptible things, as silver and gold, from your vain conversation received by tradition from your fathers; But WITH THE PRECIOUS BLOOD OF CHRIST, as of a lamb without blemish and without spot:

    1 Peter 1:18-19

I remember a brother who desperately needed a blood transfusion. This fellow was dying because of a lack of blood. I decided to get the blood myself from the blood bank. When I entered the blood bank, I noticed blood in packets lying everywhere. There was some blood on the table and there was also blood in the fridge. I looked into the fridge myself and saw several shelves laden with blood. But there was a problem. They did not have the right blood for my friend. My friend's blood was simply not available.

"Sorry, we don't have the type of blood that you need," they said.

I asked, "What do you mean by that? What kind of blood is this that is lying on the table? There are blood packets everywhere. Is this animal blood? Is it the blood of goats or the blood of bulls?"

"We don't have goat blood here!" They exclaimed. "Goat blood does not go with human blood."

Your friend needs a special type of human blood which we do not have.

Then I asked about the blood on the table. They said, *"This blood has expired.* It cannot be used any more."

"What do you mean by 'expired'?" I asked.

"It is too old," they said. "It has lost its power."

"Wow, " I thought to myself. "Then the blood of Jesus is really powerful, to have lasted for more than two thousand years without losing its power."

That night I realized how true it was that there were different kinds of blood. There were many kinds of blood but none of them was appropriate. That night I realized that all the blood in the bank could not save my friend. It was simply not the right kind of blood. It was either expired blood, or the wrong kind of blood. I began to make calls to other hospitals to see if I could find some appropriate blood for my friend.

You see, dear brother, the blood of bulls and goats could never have the power to save you from your sins. Only the blood of the sinless Lamb of God had the power to wash away sins.

This is why we sing about the blood of Jesus. This is why we sing, "There is power, power, wonder working power in the blood of the Lamb."

This is why we also sing that the blood will never lose its power. The blood of Jesus will last forever. It is eternal blood and it will always have the power to wash away sins.

2. **The blood has the supernatural power to save you from your well-deserved punishment.**

We all deserve to be punished for our sins. There is none amongst us that is innocent. No one can claim that he does not deserve to go to hell. So, what can deliver us from the punishment we deserve? Only the blood of Jesus can miraculously save us from our well-deserved punishment.

The Murderer and His Son

One day I visited a high security prison in Africa. I was slated to preach to prisoners on death row that morning. Everybody in the section I went to was condemned to death. I was met at the sectional gate of that prison by a bible-wielding gentleman who introduced himself as the leader of the prisoners' fellowship. He looked and sounded like any ordinary pastor you would meet in a church. I asked him who he was.

He said, "I'm the leader of the fellowship of the condemned cells. I was amazed that such a spiritual, bible-wielding person would be in this place. I gathered courage and asked him, "What did you do that brought you to this prison?"

He smiled sheepishly at me and said, "Oh, murder. Everyone in this section has been convicted of murder."

I was silent for a while and wondered how such a nice person could kill anyone.

Then I asked him, "Whom did you kill?"

He said, "I killed my son."

"Mercy!" I thought. "How awful."

The fellowship leader then escorted me to the meeting place. The hall was filled with sincere looking men who were praying earnestly to God. Suddenly, I was gripped with a strong desire to set them free. I felt in my heart that these were good people who had repented of their mistakes. I wanted to rush to the main gate and command that the prisoners be set free. It was then that I realized that I had no power to set these men free from their punishment. No matter what I thought and no matter how much money I had, I simply could not get them out of jail.

I thought of how difficult it would be to get a presidential pardon for the entire fellowship of murderers that had attended my service. They were in there for life and most of them would have to while away their time on earth in that prison.

That's when I realized how powerful the Blood of Jesus was. The blood of Jesus has been able to set us free from our well-deserved punishment which is an eternity in hell.

We deserve to be bound in the devil's chains! We deserve to drown in our sins! We were guilty of all the charges! We deserve to go to hell! We deserve to burn in hell!

So what has the power to change our destiny? What can get us out of eternal prison? Only something extremely powerful could work out deliverance for you and me. After all, we are clearly guilty and there is no argument about that.

The thing with the ability to free us from our well-deserved punishment is the Blood of Jesus Christ. The blood of Jesus is the only thing with that kind of power. That is why we sing the song "What can wash away my sins; Nothing but the blood of Jesus! What can make me whole again? Nothing but the blood of Jesus!"

What has the power to save us from our wretched existence as prisoners? Indeed, the blood of Jesus is powerful and supernatural!

3. The blood of Jesus has the supernatural power to prevent death.

For the life of the flesh is in the blood: and I have given it to you upon the altar to make an atonement for your souls:

Leviticus 17:11

The Blood of Jesus has within it a supernatural ability to prevent death. The blood of Jesus has within it a supernatural ability to prevent you from going to hell. The life is in the blood and therefore the absence of life-giving blood causes death.

Medical science has discovered that any part of the human body that is deprived of blood dies. For instance, sections of the brain tissue die when the blood supply to that part of the brain is blocked. This is what we call a stroke. Sections of the world are condemned to death when the Blood of Jesus is stopped from flowing there. Entire regions of the world are condemned to death and hell because no evangelist was able to go there. Life will come to the regions which receive the blood of Jesus.

The Leg Which Died

Years ago, I was in a consulting room of the hospital and my professor called me in to see a man whose leg was 'dead'. The man's leg had turned black and cold because the blood supply to the leg had been cut off in an accident.

This was the first time I had seen anything like that. I did not know that a section of the body could actually die and still be attached to the body. This man was in danger of developing gangrene in the dead leg, which would spread and kill him quickly. He had to have his leg amputated because blood had stopped flowing into it. Just as the blood was prevented from flowing into a section of that man's body, the Blood of Jesus is prevented from flowing to some sections of our world. There are sections of the world that are dominated by religions that prevent the preaching of the gospel and the reading of the bible. By their actions, they actually prevent the blood of Jesus from flowing to entire regions of the world.

That is why I am a preacher: to make the blood of Jesus avail for the souls of this world! I preach so that the blood of Jesus and the sacrifice of the cross will not be wasted. What life will come to those who know about the blood of Jesus? What a great deliverance the multitudes will have when they know about the blood of Jesus Christ!

4. **The blood of Jesus has supernatural power to bring you back from the dead.**

Now the God of peace, that BROUGHT AGAIN FROM THE DEAD our Lord Jesus, that great shepherd of the sheep, THROUGH THE BLOOD of the everlasting covenant,

Hebrews 13:20

The scripture teaches us that the blood of Jesus is the power that raised Jesus from the dead. The blood of Jesus has the power to raise the dead. It is the only power that could raise Jesus Christ out of the grave. It is by this same power of the blood that you will be raised from the dead. You will die, but you will not remain dead because of the power of the blood of Jesus.

Blood has the power to bring back people from the dead. Even natural blood does that. That is why there are blood banks. These banks store blood so that blood can be accessed quickly in emergencies to bring people back to life.

The Woman who Was Brought Back from the Dead

In medical school, I was privileged to be taught by a famous gynaecologist. After an operation, we would sit around him in the changing room while he taught us. Sometimes we wrote notes and sometimes we just listened to his amazing stories.

One day, he told us about an experience he had whilst working in the rural areas. He described a lady who had a ruptured ectopic pregnancy, was bleeding internally and was very near death.

"I was desperate," he said, "and there was no anaesthetist to make this woman sleep whilst I operated on her.

There was also no blood to transfuse her with and I knew she was dying." But life is in the blood!

Desperate situations require desperate measures! Extremes must sometimes be fought with extremes! He described how he operated on her without anaesthesia and "plugged" the source of bleeding within her abdomen. She was losing blood and she was losing her life.

After he stopped the bleeding, he realised that most of the lady's blood had collected in her abdomen. This lady had bled so much that she needed blood desperately or she would die. Life is in the blood! Since she was virtually dead, he decided to give her *her own blood*. He told us how he scooped out the lady's blood, put it in a bottle and connected it to the lady. He transfused her with *her own blood* that had leaked out. We, the students, were awe-struck as he described how the lady came back to life as her own blood re-entered her circulatory system. You see, *the life is in the blood!* As the lady's blood re-entered her she came back to life. The blood prevented the death of this woman and brought her back from the dead. The blood of Jesus will prevent eternal death and bring you back from the dead.

5. **The blood of Jesus has the supernatural ability to open the gates of heaven.**

   After this I beheld, and, lo, A GREAT MULTITUDE, which no man could number, of all nations, and kindreds, and people, and tongues, stood before the throne, and before the Lamb, clothed with white robes, and palms in their hands;

   And cried with a loud voice, saying, Salvation to our God which sitteth upon the throne, and unto the Lamb....

   And one of the elders answered, saying unto me, WHAT ARE THESE WHICH ARE ARRAYED IN WHITE ROBES? and whence came they?

And I said unto him, Sir, thou knowest. And he said to me, THESE ARE THEY which came out of great tribulation, and HAVE WASHED THEIR ROBES, and made them white IN THE BLOOD OF THE LAMB.

Revelation 7:9-10, 13-14

Indeed, one of the wonders of heaven is about how people like us could get into a place like heaven?

How did we escape the prison we deserved to go to? How did we get out of the company of fellow murderers and fellow fornicators?

How did we weave our way out of the sentence of death against us? How did we avoid the verdict of hell?

Who do we know who made a way for us to come to heaven? Which important person chipped in a word on our behalf? What are people like us doing in heaven?

Where are our dirty clothes and filthy rags? How come we are dressed in white? Do we not belong to the company of thieves, murderers and evil-doers?

How come we are singing hymns? How did people who once rejected God come to heaven? Are they there on a visit? Are they going to be here forever?

But one of the elders has the answer to all these questions. One of the elders explains that the multitudes have been able to come to heaven by washing their robes in the blood of the lamb.

The Anointed Car

One day, a great man of God visited our country. After the program, thousands of people thronged him and a large security force had to help the man of God enter the waiting limousine. Everyone wanted to get a glimpse of the man of God or even to touch the hem of his garment.

Eventually this man was whisked away by the driver and the host Bishop. Sitting in front of the car was one extra person. Who was this extra person and how did he get to be in the car when thousands of people just wanted to get a glimpse of him?

Who was the fourth man in the car? It was no other person than 'yours truly'- myself! People always wondered how I got into such a privileged position. How did I enter the anointed car? I had the ride of a lifetime as well as a most important time of fellowship and impartation of the Spirit. It was a momentous occasion for me and I received a great anointing from one of God's generals just two weeks before he died. People asked, 'How did you get into such a privileged and holy spot?' That's my secret.

Perhaps another question to ask is, "How did someone like you get into a church? How did someone like you become a minister of the gospel? What on earth is someone like you doing in a Holy place?

The only explanation that can be given for you and I to go to a great place like heaven will be the blood of Jesus. This incredibly great privilege is given to us by the blood of Jesus! One day I hope to stand in heaven. Like everybody else I will be asked why the gates of heaven should be opened unto me. I do not hope to enter heaven because I was a pastor or because I preached to large crowds. I hope to enter the gates of heaven for the same reason as everybody else – the blood of Jesus! It is the blood of Jesus that we depend on for the opening of heaven's gate.

6. **The blood of Jesus has the supernatural power to overcome the devil.**

And they OVERCAME HIM BY THE BLOOD OF THE LAMB, and by the word of their testimony; and they loved not their lives unto the death.

Revelation 12:11

41

The blood of Jesus has power. Through the blood of Jesus you will gain superiority over the devil and you will defeat him! Through the blood of Jesus you will win all the battles of life and ministry. Through the blood of Jesus you will deal with all the demonic problems of this world.

It is time to overpower and overwhelm the devil through the powerful, precious and everlasting blood of Jesus.

We live in a world dominated by an evil spirit of pride, rebellion and wickedness. This evil spirit is assisted by thousands of demons with the same evil character. All the struggles of our lives are related to the presence of evil spirits in the atmosphere. The atmosphere in different parts of the country and different parts of the world are determined by these evil spirits.

The scripture has good news for us. We can overcome the devil and his cohorts. We have been told exactly how we will overcome the devil – through the blood of Jesus.

CHAPTER 8

How the Blood Gives You Access to God

1. The blood of Jesus enables you to enter holy places.

> And their sins and iniquities will I remember no more.
> Now where remission of these is, there is no more
> offering for sin. Having therefore, brethren, boldness
> to ENTER INTO THE HOLIEST BY THE BLOOD
> OF JESUS, By a new and living way, which he hath
> consecrated for us, through the veil, that is to say, his
> flesh; And having an high priest over the house of God
>
> Hebrews 10:17-21

Holy places are out of bounds to wicked people.
Because of your sins, you have been kept away
from holy places all your life. You have always
been excluded from the inner sanctuary because of your
wicked nature. Now, through the blood of Jesus, you will be
able to penetrate to the holiest and highest places. Through
the blood of Jesus, you can pierce the veil that has kept you
far away from holy places. You have now pierced the veil
that kept you out.

Because of the access given by the blood of Jesus, you have gained admission to the holy club. You are now a real part of the holy group. Because of the blood, you can now participate and share in holy things. What a privilege to have access through the blood of Jesus! From now on, you can go to the Holy of Holies and commune directly with God. The wall of partition has been broken down by the blood of Jesus!

2. Through the blood of Jesus you become bold in the presence of God.

And their sins and iniquities will I remember no more. Now where remission of these is, there is no more offering for sin. Having therefore, brethren, BOLDNESS TO ENTER INTO THE HOLIEST BY THE BLOOD OF JESUS, By a new and living way, which he hath consecrated for us, through the veil, that is to say, his flesh; And having an high priest over the house of God; Let us draw near with a true heart in full assurance of faith, having our hearts sprinkled from an evil conscience, and our bodies washed with pure water.

Hebrews 10:17-22

Wicked people are not bold when they are in the presence of God because of their guilt and shame. They are aware of their wickedness and have deep feelings of guilt. A great blessing that comes to you through the blood of Jesus is boldness. Your sins are washed away and the records are covered with the blood. A person who is ashamed does not come out boldly. His shame makes him timid and shy. To be bold is to have self-assurance and to be without shame in spite of your sinful past. Being bold through the blood of Jesus shows a certain fearlessness in relating to your heavenly father. You can now put aside your timidity and relate boldly with God. The blood of Jesus has wiped out the records of your sin. You are just like an angel in the presence of God because of the blood of Jesus.

3. Through the blood of Jesus you have supernatural peace.

For it pleased the Father that in him should all fulness dwell; And, having made PEACE THROUGH THE BLOOD OF

HIS CROSS, by him to reconcile all things unto himself; by him, I say, whether they be things in earth, or things in heaven. And you, that were sometime alienated and enemies in your mind by wicked works, yet now hath he reconciled in the body of his flesh through death, to present you holy and unblameable and unreproveable in his sight:

Colossians 1:19-22

Through the blood of Jesus, God has given you peace. This peace means that you enter a state of tranquility or quiet. Peace through the blood of Jesus means that you are free from disquieting or oppressive thoughts and emotions. Through the blood of Jesus, you gain peace of mind and harmony in personal relationships.

4. You can now feel the presence of God because of the blood of Jesus.

That at that time ye were without Christ, being aliens from the commonwealth of Israel, and strangers from the covenants of promise, having no hope, and without God in the world: But now in Christ Jesus ye who sometimes were far off are MADE NIGH BY THE BLOOD OF CHRIST. For he is our peace, who hath made both one, and hath broken down the middle wall of partition between us; having abolished in his flesh the enmity, even the law of commandments contained in ordinances; for to make in himself of twain one new man, so making peace; And that he might reconcile both unto God in one body by the cross, having slain the enmity thereby:

Ephesians 2:12-16

God has brought us near through His blood. To be brought near means to be drawn closer to something. In this case, you have been drawn closer to God through the blood. To come near someone means you can make advances towards the person whenever you want to. Through the blood of Jesus, you can make great advances towards God. To be brought near to someone means that the person will relate with you.

From now God will have many dealings with you! He will relate with you as a child and a friend.

5. Through the blood of Jesus you can now have communion with God.

The cup of blessing which we bless, is it not THE COMMUNION OF THE BLOOD of Christ? The bread which we break, is it not the communion of the body of Christ? For we being many are one bread, and one body: for we are all partakers of that one bread.

1 Corinthians 10:16-17

Communion comes to us through the blood of Jesus Christ! This means that intimacy and deep relationships come to us through the blood of Jesus Christ. Communion is the intimate fellowship that we have with the Lord and other brethren through the blood of Jesus. It was when I found Christ that I had meaningful intimate relationships with other Christians. The communion and fellowship I found in Christ is one of the most precious gifts I have enjoyed by being born again. Many people in the world do not have great intimate relationships. Worldly relationships are usually based on money, power or sex. These worldly relationships often end up in disaster. Through the blood of Jesus, we are privileged to enjoy a special kind of relationship. It is called 'communion through the blood'. We are linked through the blood of Jesus.

In the human body, the toes, the kidneys, the heart and the brain are linked by blood. In the same way, the blood of Jesus links us with God and with the rest of the body of Christ. Through the blood of Jesus, we have communion with God and a relationship with other members of the body of Christ. Communion through the blood of Jesus Christ! Intimacy through the blood of Jesus Christ! Fellowship through the blood of Jesus Christ!

6. Through the blood of Jesus, we have a covenant with God.

He that despised Moses' law died without mercy under two or three witnesses: Of how much sorer punishment, suppose ye, shall he be thought worthy, who hath trodden under foot the Son of God, and hath counted the BLOOD OF THE COVENANT, wherewith he was sanctified, an unholy thing, and hath done despite unto the Spirit of grace?

Hebrews 10:28-29

Now the God of peace, that brought again from the dead our Lord Jesus, that great shepherd of the sheep, through THE BLOOD OF THE EVERLASTING COVENANT.

Hebrews 13:20

The blood of Jesus is called the blood of the covenant. This is because we are now able to actually have a covenant with God. Imagine that! A real agreement and covenant between a wretched sinner and Almighty God. This is the special advantage that you and I now have. There is now a divine contract and a solemn agreement that binds you forever to God and to heaven.

This wonderful privilege of having a covenant with God has angered Lucifer so much. He cannot believe that we will have such a relationship with Jehovah. We must value the privilege God has given to us that we might come so close to Him and have such access to Him.

CHAPTER 9

The Blood Enables You to Avoid Hell and to Enter Heaven

In the book of Revelation, we see a great multitude in heaven. This great multitude enjoying the sights and sounds of heaven amazed apostle John. He asked the angel who was taking him round where these people had come from. 'How did they get here?' he asked. The answer was simple: 'They came here through the blood of Jesus.'

Indeed, one of the wonders of heaven is about how people like us could get into a place like heaven!

How did we escape the prison we deserved to go to?

How did we get out of the company of murderers and fellow fornicators?

How did we weave our way out of the sentence of death against us?

How did we avoid the verdict of hell?

Who do we know who made a way for us to come to heaven?

Which important person chipped in a word on our behalf?

What are people like us doing in heaven?

Where are our dirty clothes and filthy rags?

How come we are dressed in white?

Is this not a company of thieves, murderers and evil-doers?

How come they are singing hymns?

How did people who hardly went to church manage to come to heaven?

Are they here on a visit?

Are they going to be here forever?

After these things I looked, and behold, A GREAT MULTITUDE, which no one could count, from every nation and *all* tribes and peoples and tongues, standing before the throne and before the Lamb, CLOTHED IN WHITE ROBES, and palm branches *were* in their hands;

and they cry out with a loud voice, saying, "Salvation to our God who sits on the throne, and to the Lamb."

And all the angels were standing around the throne and *around* the elders and the four living creatures; and they fell on their faces before the throne and worshiped God,

saying, "Amen, blessing and glory and wisdom and thanksgiving and honor and power and might, be to our God forever and ever. Amen."

And one of the elders answered, saying to me, "These who are clothed in the white robes, who are they, and from WHERE HAVE THEY COME?"

And I said to him, "My lord, you know." And he said to me, "These are the ones who come out of the great tribulation, and they have washed their robes and made them white in the blood of the Lamb.

Revelation 7:9-14 (NASB)

The souls of this world will sing praises to God for eternity because of their salvation. Today, salvation is hardly preached about in churches. Yet, salvation will be the most treasured gift that Christians will sing about if they make it to heaven.

Wait and see how important salvation and the blood of Jesus will be when we go out of this world. God has blessed us with salvation through the blood of Jesus.

I am a preacher to make the blood of Jesus available for all the souls of this world! I preach so that the blood of Jesus and the sacrifice of the cross will not be wasted. What praises we shall sing because of the great gift of salvation we have received through the blood of Jesus!

CHAPTER 10

How the Blood Receives its Power Through the Holy Spirit

How much more shall **THE BLOOD OF CHRIST, WHO THROUGH THE ETERNAL SPIRIT** offered himself without spot to God, purge your conscience from dead works to serve the living God?

Hebrews 9:14

The blood of Jesus Christ receives its power through the Holy Spirit. The Holy Spirit is divine because the Holy Spirit is God. The Holy Spirit is an eternal spirit. Anything the Holy Spirit is involved with is both eternal and divine. This is why the blood of Jesus Christ was offered up through the eternal spirit. Because of the association of the blood of Jesus with the Holy Spirit, the blood of Jesus becomes both an eternal and a divine thing. There are three main ways which the Holy Spirit works through the blood of Jesus.

1. The Holy Spirit imparts a *divine* value to the blood of Jesus.

The blood of Jesus Christ receives a divine value by being associated with the Holy Spirit. The blood of Jesus works through the Holy Spirit and therefore the effect of the blood is divine. The blood is no longer just a natural substance, but a divine substance. God and His power are working within that blood to save, heal and do supernatural things. "How much more shall THE BLOOD OF CHRIST, WHO THROUGH THE ETERNAL SPIRIT offered himself without spot to God, purge your conscience from dead works to serve the living God?" (Hebrews 9:14).

2. The eternal Holy Spirit imparts *eternal* value to the blood of Jesus.

The blood of Jesus Christ receives an eternal character and value because it is associated with the Holy Spirit. the blood of Jesus actually works through the Holy Spirit. The blood of Jesus is offered through the eternal spirit. Instead of the blood of Jesus decomposing and decaying it became a living and eternal thing because of its association with the Holy Spirit. As you know, the power of the Holy Spirit is eternal. The power of the Holy Spirit is the greatest power in the universe. The eternal nature of the Spirit speaks about a power that will always continue and have no end. The blood of Jesus gives an eternal redemption because it is associated with an Eternal Spirit.

Neither by the blood of goats and calves, but by his own blood he entered in once into the holy place, having obtained ETERNAL REDEMPTION for us.

Hebrews 9:12

For by one offering he hath PERFECTED FOR EVER them that are sanctified.

Hebrews 10:14

3. The Holy Spirit brought about the shedding of the blood of Jesus.

The blood of Jesus was shed with the help of the eternal spirit. The scripture teaches that the blood of Christ was offered through the eternal spirit. It is the Holy Spirit who worked out all the circumstances that resulted in Jesus being crucified and His blood being shed. The Holy Spirit is the mighty power of God that strengthened Jesus Christ during His suffering and crucifixion. The Holy Spirit is the one who helped Jesus to endure the pain of the cross. The Holy Spirit is the one who helped Jesus not to react when He was being humiliated and tortured. Jesus could have shown His power and demonstrated that He was the son of God at any point in time. Somehow, He survived extreme provocation and temptation and was able to shed His blood for mankind. This blood of Jesus Christ was shed through the help of the eternal Holy Spirit. Always remember that the blood of Jesus Christ was shed through the power of the Holy Spirit. "How much more shall THE BLOOD OF CHRIST, WHO THROUGH THE ETERNAL SPIRIT offered himself without spot to God, purge your conscience from dead works to serve the living God?" (Hebrews 9:14).

CHAPTER 11

How the Spirit and the Blood Work Together to Accomplish the Same Things

In this chapter, you will notice that many of the things that the blood of Jesus does are also done by the Spirit. This is how we know that both the Spirit and the blood work together to accomplish great things for God. The blood of Jesus and the spirit of God are completely united in the spiritual work that they do.

1. **Both the blood and the Spirit agree and are united in their work.**

   And there are three that bear witness in earth, the Spirit, and the water, and the blood: and these three agree in one.

   1 John 5:8

2. **Both the Spirit and the blood give life.**

   Whoso eateth my flesh, and DRINKETH MY BLOOD, HATH ETERNAL LIFE; and I will raise him up at the last day.

   John 6:54

It is THE SPIRIT THAT QUICKENETH; the flesh profiteth nothing: the words that I speak unto you, they are spirit, and they are life.

John 6:63

3. Both the Spirit and the blood bring you near to God.

But now in Christ Jesus ye who sometimes were far off are MADE NIGH BY THE BLOOD of Christ.

Ephesians 2:13

For through him we both have ACCESS BY ONE SPIRIT unto the Father.

Ephesians 2:18

4. Despising the Spirit and despising the blood are seen as one and the same thing.

Of how much sorer punishment, suppose ye, shall he be thought worthy, who hath trodden under foot the Son of God, and hath COUNTED THE BLOOD of the covenant, wherewith he was sanctified, AN UNHOLY THING, AND HATH DONE DESPITE UNTO THE SPIRIT OF GRACE?

Hebrews 10:29

Why the Work of the Holy Spirit Follows the Work of the Blood

1. The outpouring of the blood of Jesus on Calvary's cross made it possible for the outpouring of the Spirit at Pentecost.

The event of Jesus dying on the cross was the event in which the blood of Jesus was poured out for mankind. The event of Pentecost is the event in which the Holy Ghost was poured out on all flesh. Pentecost happened a few weeks after Calvary.

> But ye shall receive power, after that the Holy Ghost is come upon you: and ye shall be witnesses unto me both in Jerusalem, and in all Judaea, and in Samaria, and unto the uttermost part of the earth.
>
> Acts 1:8

2. The Lord could baptize us with the Spirit only after He had shed His blood.

Even though the disciples lived and worked closely with the Lord, Jesus could not give them the Holy Spirit until after He died. Jesus Christ longed to bless them but He could not do so until the blood was shed.

But this spake he of the Spirit, which they that believe on him should receive: for THE HOLY GHOST WAS NOT YET GIVEN; BECAUSE THAT JESUS WAS NOT YET GLORIFIED.

John 7:39

3. The Old Testament priests were anointed with the oil only after they were anointed with blood.

And he shall kill the lamb of the trespass offering, and the priest shall take *some* of the blood of the trespass offering, and put *it* upon the tip of the right ear of him that is to be cleansed, and upon the thumb of his right hand, and upon the great toe of his right foot: And the priest shall pour of the oil into the palm of his own left hand:

And the priest shall sprinkle with his right finger *some* of the oil that is in his left hand seven times before the LORD:

And the priest shall put of the oil that is in his hand upon the tip of the right ear of him that *is* to be cleansed, and upon the thumb of his right hand, and upon the great toe of his right foot, upon the place of the blood of the trespass offering:

Leviticus 14:25-28

4. John the Baptist described Jesus as doing two main things.

He proclaimed Jesus to be the one who would take away sins with His blood and baptise with the Holy Spirit.

'behold the lamb of God who taketh away the sin of the world'

John 1:29

'this is he who baptiseth with the Holy Spirit'

John 1:33

5. Both the blood and the Spirit emanate from the Lamb of God and the throne.

The seven spirits of God are sent out from the throne in which stands the lamb that was slain. The Spirit of God flows directly from the lamb who has shed His blood.

And I beheld, and, lo, in the midst of the throne and of the four beasts, and in the midst of the elders, stood A LAMB AS IT HAD BEEN SLAIN, having seven horns and seven eyes, which are THE SEVEN SPIRITS OF GOD sent forth into all the earth.

Revelation 5:6

CHAPTER 13

How the Blood Enables You to Enter the Ministry

1. Aaron and his sons entered the ministry through the blood.

Much of the consecration of Aaron and his sons had to do with sanctification and cleansing rituals through blood and sacrifice. No one is worthy to be a minister of the gospel. All that we do and accomplish for the Lord are by grace and grace alone. If you ever think that you are being used because you are worthy or you are the good type, remember that Aaron, the High Priest, and his sons entered the ministry only because of the blood. Do you want to be hallowed so that you can minister the word of God? there is only one way for you to become worthy or qualified for this great work. It is through the blood.

And THIS IS THE THING THAT THOU SHALT DO UNTO THEM TO HALLOW THEM, TO MINISTER UNTO ME in the priest's office: Take one young bullock, and two rams without blemish, And unleavened bread, and cakes unleavened tempered with oil, and wafers unleavened anointed with oil: of wheaten flour shalt thou make them.

And thou shalt put them into one basket, and bring them in the basket, with the bullock and the two rams. And Aaron and his sons thou shalt bring unto the door of the tabernacle of the congregation, and shalt wash them with water.

And thou shalt take the garments, and put upon Aaron the coat, and the robe of the ephod, and the ephod, and the breastplate, and gird him with the curious girdle of the ephod:

And thou shalt put the mitre upon his head, and put the holy crown upon the mitre.

Then shalt thou take the anointing oil, and pour it upon his head, and anoint him.

And thou shalt bring his sons, and put coats upon them. And thou shalt gird them with girdles, Aaron and his sons, and put the bonnets on them: and the priest's office shall be theirs for a perpetual statute: and thou shalt consecrate Aaron and his sons.

And thou shalt cause a bullock to be brought before the tabernacle of the congregation: and Aaron and his sons shall put their hands upon the head of the bullock.

And thou shalt kill the bullock before the LORD, by the door of the tabernacle of the congregation.

And thou shalt take of the blood of the bullock, and put it upon the horns of the altar with thy finger, and pour all the blood beside the bottom of the altar.

And thou shalt take all the fat that covereth the inwards, and the caul that is above the liver, and the two kidneys, and the fat that is upon them, and burn them upon the altar.But the flesh of the bullock, and his skin, and his dung, shalt thou burn with fire without the camp: it is a sin offering.

Thou shalt also take one ram; and Aaron and his sons shall put their hands upon the head of the ram. And thou shalt slay the ram, and thou shalt take his blood, and sprinkle it round about upon the altar. And thou shalt cut the ram in pieces, and wash the inwards of him, and his legs, and put them unto his pieces, and unto his head.

And thou shalt burn the whole ram upon the altar: it is a burnt offering unto the LORD: it is a sweet savour, an offering made by fire unto the LORD.

And thou shalt take the other ram; and Aaron and his sons shall put their hands upon the head of the ram. Then shalt thou kill the ram, and take of his blood, and put it upon the tip of the right ear of Aaron, and upon the tip of the right ear of his sons, and upon the thumb of their right hand, and upon the great toe of their right foot, and sprinkle the blood upon the altar round about. And thou shalt take of the blood that is upon the altar, and of the anointing oil, and sprinkle it upon Aaron, and upon his garments, and upon his sons, and upon the garments of his sons with him: and he shall be hallowed, and his garments, and his sons, and his sons' garments with him.

Exodus 29:1-21

2. People are made priests through the blood

In the New Testament, the method of becoming a priest is exactly the same. It is by the blood of Jesus that you can become a minister of the gospel. The blood of Jesus makes a way for unworthy people like us to be ministers. The greatest gift you have ever received is your salvation. But the greatest mind-boggling privilege you will ever receive is to be called into the service of the king. To be a minister of the gospel is the highest privilege and the greatest job you can ever be given to do. John, the revelator, explained when he said we have been made priests by the blood of Jesus. What an honour! How precious this blood must be which both saves us and also qualifies us for ministry.

And they sung a new song, saying, Thou art worthy to take the book, and to open the seals thereof: for thou wast slain, and hast redeemed us to God BY THY BLOOD out of every kindred, and tongue, and people, and nation;

AND HAST MADE US UNTO OUR GOD KINGS AND
PRIESTS: and we shall reign on the earth.

Revelation 5:9-10

3. Paul entered the ministry through the mercies of God and the blood of Jesus.

Therefore, having this ministry BY THE MERCY OF
GOD, we do not lose heart

2 Corinthians 4:1

Paul was no different from the rest of us. He was a sinner,
a blasphemer and injurious to the will of God. Yet, God called
him and made him worthy to be a minister of the gospel. The
only way apostle Paul could minister the word of God was if a
powerful cleansing agent existed. This powerful cleansing agent
would have to cleanse him of his many sins and crimes against
God and the church. Indeed, there was a powerful cleansing
agent available to cleanse Saul and make him a new creature
and a minister of the gospel. That powerful cleansing agent was
nothing other than the blood of Jesus which taketh away the sins
of the whole world. Today, the blood of Jesus is available to save
you and to prepare you to work for God in the ministry. When
you see how much mercy you have received you must never lose
heart and stop working for God.

And I thank Christ Jesus our Lord, who hath enabled
me, for that he counted me faithful, putting me into
the ministry; Who was before a blasphemer, and a
persecutor, and injurious: but I obtained mercy, because
I did it ignorantly in unbelief. And the grace of our Lord
was exceeding abundant with faith and love which is in
Christ Jesus. This is a faithful saying, and worthy of all
acceptation, that Christ Jesus came into the world to save
sinners; of whom I am chief.

Howbeit for this cause I obtained mercy, that in me first
Jesus Christ might shew forth all longsuffering, for a
pattern to them which should hereafter believe on him to

life everlasting. [17]Now unto the King eternal, immortal, invisible, the only wise God, be honour and glory for ever and ever. Amen.

1 Timothy 1:12-17